STEWARDED INFLUENCE

Faithful Leadership in a Results-Driven World

Kevin Horton

Copyright © 2026 Kevin Horton

All rights reserved.

No part of this book may be reproduced, distributed, or transmitted in any form or by any means without prior written permission from the author, except in the case of brief quotations embodied in critical reviews and other noncommercial uses permitted by copyright law.

The views expressed in this book are solely those of the author and do not reflect the views of any employer, organization, or affiliated entity.

Certain names, details, and identifying characteristics have been omitted or modified to protect the privacy of individuals and organizations. Any resemblance to specific persons or entities is unintentional.

First Edition

Published by Kevin Horton Publishing

ISBN: 979-8-9951044-0-7

Cover design by Mehrab Meraj

I thank God for every blessing in my life.

To my wife, my son, my parents, my brother, and my in-laws — your support, belief, and encouragement have sustained me more than I can express.

To the leaders who have shaped me, from my first job to corporate leadership — thank you for investing in me. This book exists because you did.

Table Of Contents

INTRODUCTION

Still Becoming

I did not write this book because I believe I have leadership figured out.

If anything, I wrote it because I have learned how much there still is to learn.

Throughout my career, I have been shaped by the leaders around me. Some were polished and articulate. Some were steady and understated. Some rose quickly. Others built influence slowly over years. Each modeled something worth observing.

I paid attention not only to what they achieved, but to how they carried themselves — how they responded under pressure, how they handled correction, how they treated people when outcomes were uncertain.

Over time, I noticed something consistent.

The leaders who endured — the ones people trusted — were not the loudest or the most celebrated. They were steady. They were consistent. They evolved. They adjusted. They did not pretend to be finished.

That realization reshaped me.

Early in my career, I assumed strong performance would naturally lead to advancement. Over time, I realized performance is only one layer. Leadership requires formation. And formation is ongoing.

There is no finished product.

Only the pursuit of it.

I am still becoming.

There are conversations I would handle differently today than I would have five years ago. There are decisions I now approach with more patience than I once did. There are moments I still replay and refine.

Leadership demands constant evolution.

The moment we believe we have arrived is often the moment growth begins to stall.

This book is not a declaration of mastery. It is a reflection on formation — on what I have observed, attempted, adjusted, and learned through seasons of responsibility and pressure.

If there is a thread that runs through these pages, it is this:

Leadership is not about arriving at a position.

It is about stewarding influence faithfully while you continue becoming.

I remain in that process.

And I suspect I always will.

01
The Call That Changed My Pace

I was inside a convenience store, mid-conversation with a customer, when my phone buzzed.

It was my boss.

Midday calls weren't unusual. I was on my route, moving store to store, checking execution, selling where I could, working through the normal rhythm of the day. I knew a decision was coming at some point, so the call itself didn't catch me off guard.

But I didn't know what it meant.

I stepped away and answered.

He got straight to it.

"They decided to go in another direction. You represented yourself well."

His tone was steady. Professional. The kind of tone that tells you the decision is final before you even process the words.

I remember thinking, *I know this isn't coming from him.* He didn't make the call. And in a strange way, I felt for him having to deliver it.

I responded the way you're supposed to. Calm. Appreciative. Professional.

Then I hung up and walked back into the store.

Nothing around me had changed. Customers were still moving through the aisles. The register was still ringing. The conversation I had stepped away from was still there waiting on me.

But internally, everything shifted.

Disappointment hit first. Then embarrassment.

I believed I was ready. I believed my performance had earned it. And now I had to finish out the day—walking into more stores, talking to more people—knowing I had been passed over.

I kept working. I finished that store. Then the next one. Then the next.

But if I'm being honest, I wasn't fully there.

My mind was somewhere else.

What did I say wrong?

What didn't I say?

Where did I miss?

Who got it?

What are people going to think?

Is this path over for me?

Those questions didn't come one at a time. They stacked. And the more they stacked, the heavier the day felt.

By the time I got home, it had turned into something worse—a full-blown internal spiral.

I talked to my parents that night. They were encouraging, steady like they've always been. They reminded me of who I was. Told me this didn't define me. Told me there would be more opportunities.

And I believed them.

But it didn't fix it.

Because encouragement doesn't replace processing. And in that moment, I was in the middle of an honest-to-goodness pity party. The kind you can't shortcut. The kind you have to work your way through.

That took time.

Over the next few days, the emotion settled enough for me to think more clearly. And when it did, I started asking a better question—not *how did I get passed over*, but *why?*

So I went digging.

What I found wasn't dramatic. It wasn't political. It wasn't anything I had said or failed to say.

The other candidate had more experience.

That was it.

At first, that almost frustrated me more. There was nothing to point to, nothing to fix in a clean, immediate way. Just a simple reality:

I needed more time.

More growth.

More development beyond performance.

That realization changed everything.

Up to that point, I had operated with a simple belief: if I performed well enough, the next opportunity would come.

And to a degree, that's true.

But performance is only part of the equation.

Performance earns entry.

Influence earns trust.

I didn't need to prove I was ready.

I needed to prepare to be ready.

That shift—from proving to preparing—changed my pace.

I stopped focusing on what I thought I had earned and started focusing on what I still needed to build.

Ironically, the person who didn't give me that role later gave me a much bigger one—one that expanded my network and stretched my leadership in ways I wasn't ready for at the time of that first opportunity.

I can still picture that store. The aisles. The register. The phone in my hand.

At the time, it felt like a closed door.

It was actually the beginning of a different pace.

02

Leading Before You're Chosen

After being passed over, I had a decision to make.

I could protect my ego, retreat into strong performance, and wait quietly for the next opportunity.

Or I could expand my influence before anyone handed me authority.

Up to that point, I believed promotion followed production. If I did my job well enough, advancement would take care of itself.

That belief wasn't entirely wrong.

But it was incomplete.

Not long after that missed opportunity, our team was introduced to a new set of performance metrics. They weren't simple. They weren't intuitive. And for a while, they became a point of frustration across the team.

People were trying to figure them out.

Trying to understand what actually moved the number.

Trying to get above target—and struggling.

I spent time digging into it.

Not because I was told to. Not because I had authority to. But because I knew if I could figure it out, it would matter.

Over time, something started to click.

I began to see patterns—what worked, what didn't, where execution broke down. And as I applied it in my own accounts, the results followed.

Quietly at first.

Then consistently.

Eventually, I started having conversations with a few teammates.

"Here's what I'm seeing."

"Here's what's actually moving it."

"Here's where I think we're missing."

At first, it felt uncomfortable.

I was still a peer. No title. No authority. No formal responsibility to coach anyone.

Just another guy on the team.

And there's a fine line in that position. You don't want to come across like you're trying to elevate yourself. You don't want to lose the locker room. You don't want people thinking, *Who does he think he is?*

I remember thinking, *This could backfire.*

This could get shut down quickly.

But it didn't.

People leaned in.

Not because I had a title.

Because it was working.

Over time, those one-off conversations turned into something more consistent. I found myself walking teammates through the metric—how to approach it, how to adjust, how to think about it differently.

Without realizing it, I had stepped into a form of leadership.

No one had given it to me.

I had chosen it.

Then came the Tuesday meetings.

Every week, we'd sit down and go through performance—what was working, what wasn't, where we stood. At some point, it became my responsibility to report out on that metric.

The first time I stood up to walk through it, I could feel it.

A few guys leaned back in their chairs. A couple looked down at their sheets. One or two were watching closely.

These were still my peers.

The same people I joked with. Rode with. Learned from.

And now I was the one leading part of the conversation.

There was a split second where the thought hit:

Is this about to change things?

Am I about to separate myself from the group?

I walked through the numbers. Kept it simple. Showed what was working. Showed where we were missing.

No one pushed back.

No one shut it down.

And when it was over, we moved on like we always did.

That was the moment.

Nothing changed.

I was still one of the guys.

Still part of the team.

Still able to contribute relationally while also contributing directionally.

That was a relief.

Because it reinforced something I hadn't fully understood before:

Leadership doesn't require distance.

It requires alignment.

As the weeks went on, the metric improved.

Not overnight. Not perfectly. But steadily.

What had been a point of confusion became a point of clarity. What had been a drag on performance became something we were managing—and eventually, something we were winning in.

And with that came something I didn't fully appreciate in the moment.

Trust.

Leadership within the organization started to notice.

Not just the result—but the role I had played in helping the team get there.

It gave them something to point to.

Something to speak to in rooms I wasn't in.

Looking back, that season marked a shift.

I stopped waiting to be chosen.

I started acting like I already was.

Within a year of being told no, I was told yes.

The promotion required relocation. A new environment. Higher expectations. Less margin for error.

But the foundation had already been set.

You can prepare for a title long before you hold it.

You can lead before you are chosen.

And the leaders worth following are often the ones who practiced influence quietly—before it was ever required publicly.

03

Building It the First Time

My first leadership role was not defined by crisis.

It was defined by construction.

I stepped into a new location knowing no one well. I had earned the promotion, but I had not earned their trust. Authority had changed overnight.

Credibility had not.

I knew I was capable.

I believed I could do the job.

But belief doesn't carry weight with a new team.

You have to prove it.

I had to show leadership I was capable—that I was deserving of the opportunity they had given me.

And I had to show the team something even more important:

That they could trust me.

That following me would benefit them.

That I wasn't just another person passing through with a title.

My boss spent the first couple of days taking me around, introducing me to each team member one-on-one.

Those conversations were fine on the surface.

But internally, I was processing more than I let on.

I'm naturally introverted. Meeting new people doesn't come easy to me. I've grown in that area over time, but my default is still the same—I'm just as comfortable in silence as I am in conversation, especially with people I don't know well.

So while we were talking, I was also thinking.

Am I supposed to be coaching right now—or just getting to know them?

Is he evaluating me while I'm trying to figure them out?

Am I saying enough? Too much?

There was a constant stream of questions running in the background.

And when your mind is that active, it's hard to be fully present.

Looking back, I'm sure some of those early interactions weren't as natural as they could have been. Some probably got an incomplete picture of who I was.

That was part of the process.

There wasn't a single moment where I felt tested.

It was a series of them.

Questions came steadily.

"What would you do if this happened?"

"How would you handle this situation?"

"What would you say if a customer pushed back like this?"

They weren't disrespectful.

But they were deliberate.

They were trying to figure out who I was as a leader—how I thought, how I responded, how I handled pressure.

And I understood that.

Because if the roles were reversed, I would have done the same thing.

One of the first moments that made the weight of the role real came through a hiring decision.

We had an open position.

Several candidates were strong.

The process required clarity. It required fairness. It required alignment with my senior leader.

But ultimately, it required a decision.

And that decision meant someone was going to hear no.

I called the candidate into the office and sat down across from them.

I've always believed in handling those conversations face to face.

It's not the easy route.

But it's the right one.

I had been on the other side of that moment before—getting news like that delivered by someone who had no real connection to the decision. It felt distant. Impersonal. Final without explanation.

I wasn't going to do that to someone else.

People deserve to hear directly from the person making the decision.

They deserve clarity.

They deserve respect.

So I walked through it with them.

Why we made the decision. What went into it. Where they stood.

They weren't happy.

I didn't expect them to be.

And I didn't blame them.

Moments like that aren't about being liked. They're about being clear and being fair.

At the same time, I knew I had made the right call.

And that's the tension in leadership.

You can be confident in the decision—and still feel the weight of delivering it.

After the conversation, I sat in my car and replayed it.

Not the outcome.

The delivery.

Was I clear?

Was I steady?

Did I handle that the right way?

Leadership doesn't end when the meeting ends.

It lingers.

Those early weeks required constant adjustment.

When I was a peer, I could speak freely. Now, people listened differently. Not just for ideas—but for direction.

Tone mattered more.

Pace mattered more.

Consistency mattered more.

At the same time, the team gave me something I didn't expect.

They pushed me.

They tested me.

But they also allowed me to grow.

They allowed me to try—and succeed.

They allowed me to try—and fail.

They extended grace.

Not lowered standards.

Not indifference.

Grace.

Over time, something shifted.

The questions became less frequent.

The conversations became more open.

The skepticism softened into trust.

We started building something steady.

And we built it together.

I'm still close with many of those team members to this day.

I'm grateful for what they taught me.

And I'm hopeful that some of what I tried to teach them stayed with them as well.

That first leadership role didn't make me impressive.

It made me intentional.

04
Pressure, Pace, and Private Frustration

The early months in the new role were uneven.

We were trying to build something, but it wasn't consistent yet. Execution wavered. Priorities blurred at times. We were preparing for the next year, talking through how we would get off to a strong start, but I hadn't fully found my rhythm yet.

I was still adjusting.

To the role.

To the expectations.

To the environment outside of work.

That day, we had a planned meeting focused on the upcoming year—what needed to improve, how we were going to elevate performance, how we were going to start strong.

By the time it wrapped up, I was tired.

Mid-afternoon. Long day. A lot of conversation.

I was ready to get in the car and make the drive home.

We stepped outside to the valet area. Cars moving. Noise in the background. The kind of environment where your guard is down because the day feels like it's already over.

My senior leader walked out with me.

There was a brief buildup.

"How's it going?"

"What did you think of the meeting?"

Normal conversation.

Then it shifted.

"You need to lead more. And you need to lead better. You need to do it now."

It was direct.

Matter-of-fact.

No raised voice. No drawn-out explanation.

Just clarity—with a little edge to it.

I didn't say much back.

He was the boss.

And truthfully, I knew I could do better.

But internally, it hit hard.

I was frustrated.

Defensive.

You don't see everything I'm doing.

I'm still trying to figure this out.

There's more going on than you realize.

I thought he had some nerve to just put it out there like that.

The timing.

The delivery.

The lack of context.

It didn't sit well.

And if I'm honest, I justified it to myself as I walked to my car.

All the reasons.

All the explanations.

Everything that wasn't being seen.

But underneath all of that, there was something else.

I hadn't hit my stride yet.

I hadn't shown my best.

And I knew it.

That's what made it hard to ignore.

Because even if I didn't like how it was delivered…

It was right.

The drive home gave me time to work through it.

At first, the frustration stayed close to the surface.

Replaying the moment.

Replaying the tone.

Replaying what I wished I had said.

But somewhere along the way, the conversation shifted.

From frustration…

To urgency.

I realized something I hadn't fully accepted yet.

My personal situation—being new to the area, not knowing anyone outside of work, not having a rhythm yet—that was real.

But it wasn't relevant to performance.

Not in the eyes of leadership.

And not in the reality of the role.

That wasn't an excuse.

It was a responsibility.

I needed to deal with it.

And I did.

But it couldn't interfere with the task at hand.

That drive forced a decision.

I could keep justifying where I was…

Or I could take ownership of where I needed to go.

That's where the shift happened.

Not emotional.

Not dramatic.

Just clear.

I needed to lead more.

I needed to lead better.

And I needed to do it now.

From that point forward, the urgency changed.

The focus sharpened.

The standard elevated.

Not because of how the message was delivered—

But because of what it exposed.

That moment taught me something I've carried with me ever since:

Frustration expressed publicly often multiplies confusion.

Processed privately, it can create clarity.

There were other conversations like that.

Moments where expectations were raised. Where feedback came direct.
Where I was pushed beyond where I was comfortable.

I didn't always like how it was delivered.

But I learned to separate the message from the delivery.

And more importantly, I learned to choose where my response showed up.

Because the team would feel it.

If I carried frustration into conversations, it would spread.

If I reacted emotionally, it would create instability.

But if I processed it privately and showed up steady, it gave the team something to follow.

The team should feel urgency.

Not volatility.

That distinction became foundational.

The lesson from that afternoon stayed with me.

Lead more.

Lead better.

Lead now.

05
Vision Simplified

Vision is often misunderstood.

In many organizations, it becomes a repackaging of priorities—polished language, layered slides, ambitious targets. It sounds strong. It feels important.

But it rarely feels clear.

When vision is complex, it becomes noise.

And when it becomes noise, execution slows.

Early in my leadership tenure, I felt that tension.

There were always multiple priorities. Multiple initiatives. Multiple conversations pulling in different directions. Everything mattered—at least it sounded like it did.

And when everything matters, nothing gets the attention it should.

Meetings would drift.

Conversations would expand.

Execution would follow wherever the most recent message pointed.

It wasn't a lack of effort.

It was a lack of clarity.

So I decided to simplify it.

The first time I introduced what would become "the page," we were in a small conference room. The team was seated, focused, waiting to see where we were headed.

I pulled it up on the screen.

No elaborate build-up.

No extended explanation.

Just a single page.

"This is where we're going to focus," I told them.

It wasn't complicated.

Six to eight priorities, divided in half.

Three or four at the top—primary. Nonnegotiable. If we did nothing else, we would do these well.

The rest below—still important, but never at the expense of the primary.

It was rooted in the organization's priorities.

But it was simplified on purpose.

I wanted them to move faster.

More intentionally.

More deliberately.

I didn't want them guessing what mattered.

I wanted them knowing.

The initial reaction in the room was steady.

No pushback.

No resistance.

Just attention.

They understood it.

And more importantly, they could see it.

But the real test didn't come in that room.

It came afterward.

Because simplicity, when it replaces complexity, creates tension.

Not because it's wrong.

But because it's different.

Other teams pushed back.

Not directly at first.

More through questions.

More through comparison.

More through the weight of "this isn't how we've always done it."

There's comfort in complexity.

It allows for flexibility.

It allows for movement.

It allows for explanation when things don't go as planned.

Simplicity removes that.

It forces decisions.

It exposes trade-offs.

And it requires discipline.

There were moments when conversations started to drift.

New ideas. New initiatives. New directions.

And I would bring it back.

"Is it on the page?"

At first, that question came from me.

A way to anchor the conversation.

A way to filter noise.

But over time, something shifted.

The team started asking it.

In meetings.

In conversations.

In decision-making.

"Is it on the page?"

I remember one meeting where a new idea was gaining traction—good idea, strong case, the kind of thing that usually would have turned into another priority.

Before I could say anything, someone on the team spoke up.

"Is it on the page?"

The room paused.

We looked at it.

It wasn't.

And just like that, the conversation shifted.

Not dismissed.

Not ignored.

Just aligned.

That was the moment it clicked.

Not when I introduced it.

Not when I explained it.

But when they owned it.

When it became part of how they thought—not just what they were told.

From that point forward, everything tightened.

Meetings became more efficient.

Decisions became faster.

Execution became more consistent.

Not because we were doing more.

Because we were doing less—better.

The simplicity didn't limit the team.

It freed them.

It removed hesitation.

It reduced second-guessing.

It created alignment without constant direction.

And over time, the results followed.

Month after month.

Year after year.

Consistently near the top across scorecards and trackers.

Not because we chased everything.

Because we focused on what mattered most.

At some point, everyone saw it.

What may have looked like an oversimplification at first…

Was actually discipline.

Vision should not overwhelm.

It should clarify.

It should reduce friction.

It should make the path obvious.

Leadership is not about saying more.

It is about saying what matters most—

And having the discipline to stay there.

06
Accountability Without Volatility

Accountability often carries a negative tone.

It can feel confrontational. Heavy. Uncomfortable.

Handled correctly, it is stabilizing.

It keeps teams aligned. It protects standards. It reinforces clarity.

It only becomes corrosive when it is inconsistent—or delivered with volatility.

I've had this conversation many times.

Different people. Different situations.

But the pattern is usually the same.

Something isn't being executed.

Inventory isn't managed correctly. Orders are off. Waste creeps in.
Processes are ignored. Distractions take priority.

At first, it's a conversation.

Then another.

Then a more direct one.

And when it shows up again after that, frustration builds.

That's the moment that matters.

Because that's the moment where your response either helps the
situation—or makes it worse.

I've felt it.

The urge to erupt.

We've already talked about this.

This shouldn't be this hard.

Why are we still here?

Those thoughts come quickly.

And if you bring them into the room, they take over the conversation.

That's why I learned to deal with them before I ever sat down across from someone.

Most of that happened in my truck.

Before the conversation.

Door closed. No audience. No filter.

I would say everything I wanted to say.

Out loud.

Not to them.

But to myself.

All the frustration.

All the irritation.

Everything I would never say to another person.

Not because it wasn't real.

But because it wouldn't be productive.

You have to get that out of the way.

Because once you walk into the room, the goal isn't to release frustration.

It's to create clarity.

By the time I sat down with them, the tone was different.

Calm.

Direct.

Clear.

I didn't avoid the issue.

I framed it.

"Here's what we've talked about."

"Here's what we expect."

"Here's where you're still falling short."

"Here's what needs to change."

"And here's what happens if it doesn't."

No yelling.

No escalation.

No theatrics.

Just clarity.

Most people already know how the conversation is going to go before it starts.

If you've had informal conversations, then formal ones, and the issue still shows up, they're walking in expecting it to be bad.

And more often than not, they're expecting anger.

That's what they've seen before.

That's what they've experienced elsewhere.

But anger doesn't help people get better.

Clarity does.

Direction does.

Directness does.

I remember one conversation where, toward the end, they paused and said,

"I thought this was going to be worse."

That stuck with me.

Not because I had avoided the issue.

But because I had handled it the right way.

There were times when people responded to that.

They improved.

Not immediately.

Not perfectly.

But consistently.

Because they knew exactly where they stood.

And they knew exactly what to do.

There were other times when they didn't.

And the outcome was different.

We had to part ways.

That's part of leadership too.

Accountability doesn't always lead to improvement.

Sometimes it leads to separation.

But even in those moments, the standard remains.

You don't degrade people.

You don't dehumanize them.

You don't let frustration turn into disrespect.

Because leadership isn't just about holding people accountable.

It's about how you do it.

The conversation doesn't start when you sit down.

It starts before that.

In the quiet moments where you decide what kind of leader you're going to be when it matters.

And for me, that decision became clear.

Accountability should feel structured.

Not emotional.

Firm.

Not volatile.

Because the goal isn't to win the moment.

It's to improve the person—or make the right decision if they won't.

07
Ego and Quiet Insecurity

Ego is not always loud.

Sometimes it fills the room — needing the last word, holding the floor too long, insisting on control.

Other times, it is quieter.

It shows up in subtle ways — in how tightly we grip an opinion, in how quickly we dismiss an alternative, in how reluctant we are to admit uncertainty. Teams notice those moments.

When being right becomes more important than getting it right, something begins to fracture. Collaboration narrows. Creativity tightens. Culture erodes slowly, not suddenly.

I have seen ego derail strong teams.

But if I am honest, my struggle has rarely been loud ego.

It has been quiet insecurity.

I am aware of how destructive ego can be, and at times that awareness caused me to swing too far in the opposite direction. I hesitated to speak boldly about wins. I avoided spotlight. I downplayed contributions.

In one of our anonymous team surveys, that came back clearly.

Team members shared that they wished I would be louder about accomplishments — not for recognition, but because they believed credit was deserved.

I remember reading that and sitting with it longer than I expected.

My first instinct was to dismiss it.

That's not the kind of leader I want to be.

I don't need attention.

The work should speak for itself.

But the more I thought about it, the more I realized something I hadn't fully considered.

It wasn't about me.

It was about them.

By holding back, I wasn't protecting humility.

I was limiting clarity.

I was muting momentum.

There were moments in meetings where progress had been made — real progress — and instead of reinforcing it, I moved on too quickly. Instead of highlighting what was working, I stayed quiet to avoid drawing attention.

In doing that, I thought I was staying grounded.

In reality, I was missing an opportunity to lead.

Humility is not invisibility.

Avoiding ego does not require shrinking.

Leadership requires clarity of voice.

Insecurity can distort judgment just as much as arrogance can. It can cause hesitation when conviction is needed. It can mute a message that should be delivered plainly. It can delay decisions out of fear of being wrong.

The goal is not dominance.

It is balance.

Strength is not self-sufficiency. It is dependence rightly placed.

Over time, I have learned that alignment matters more than attention. Influence matters more than applause.

But influence requires presence.

It requires a voice that is willing to step forward when it matters.

When ego is quiet — in either direction — teams function better.

Leadership is not about controlling the room.

It is about stewarding it.

08
Playing the Long Game

We live in a culture that rewards acceleration.

Faster promotions. Faster recognition. Faster visible proof that something is happening.

But leadership rarely unfolds at that pace.

It forms slowly, often invisibly.

Early in my career, I realized I would likely spend two or more years in most roles I held. That realization changed how I approached them. If I was going to be there for a while, I might as well build something durable.

I stopped thinking in quarters and started thinking in cycles.

CHAPTER 08

It is one thing to have a strong year. It is another to sustain performance — to build systems, relationships, and rhythms that endure beyond a single season. A highlight year can happen. Durable leadership requires deeper roots.

There were seasons when I lived farther from home than I wanted.

That distance mattered more than I expected.

I found myself looking for ways to get closer — not one specific role, but almost anything that would allow me to make that move. I was open to different paths, different responsibilities, different directions if it meant being nearer to what was familiar.

At the time, it felt practical.

It felt justified.

But looking back, I wasn't considering something important.

I wasn't considering that I might be trying to move faster than I was being formed.

I was focused on proximity.

Not alignment.

Opportunities closer to home surfaced, and I pursued them in quiet conversations. I never formally applied, but the interest was there. The desire was real.

And each time, the answer came back the same.

It wasn't the right fit.

At first, that answer felt frustrating.

Restrictive.

Like something was being held back.

But over time, it became clear that something else was happening.

I was trying to force a path that wasn't meant for me in that season.

I was trying to solve for comfort, not calling.

When those doors didn't open, I stayed where I was.

And I kept building.

Then something shifted.

A different opportunity came.

A better one.

One that expanded my scope, stretched my leadership, and aligned with what I had been building — not what I had been chasing.

It didn't feel forced.

It didn't require maneuvering.

It came together with a clarity that was different from everything I had pursued before.

And that's when it clicked.

When things fall into place without being forced, there is often alignment behind them.

Not ease.

Not absence of challenge.

But alignment.

What I had missed earlier was that access is not the same as alignment.

Just because something is available does not mean it is right.

Acceleration, detached from formation, rarely produces durability.

Playing the long game requires patience — and patience rarely feels glamorous. It often feels quiet. Unnoticed. Slow.

But over time, it builds credibility that acceleration alone cannot.

None of this eliminated ambition.

It refined it.

Instead of asking how quickly I could move, I began asking how fully I could maximize the role I held.

That shift changed my pace.

09
Leading When Life Doesn't Pause

When COVID disrupted the world, it disrupted leadership in ways none of us had rehearsed.

My role was not designed to be remote. It required presence — store visits, ride-alongs, in-person meetings, visible momentum. Almost overnight, I was working from home.

At the same time, my wife was pregnant.

The world felt uncertain. The routines that had anchored work were gone. Conversations shifted from growth and execution to safety and stability. Expectations changed — not in ambition, but in realism.

The company was empathetic. Supportive. Expectations shifted from high-level execution to survival — literally and metaphorically. We were not pretending nothing had changed. We were navigating something none of us had led through before.

Still, responsibility remained.

There were weeks when half the team was out.

Illness. Quarantine. Family needs.

We were constantly adjusting — coverage plans changing, priorities shifting, trying to keep things moving with limited visibility and even less stability.

I remember one stretch where it felt like everything was in motion at once.

People out.

Plans changing.

Communication constant but never quite enough.

At the same time, I was carrying the reality at home — preparing for a child in the middle of uncertainty, trying to balance what was happening personally with what was required professionally.

It wasn't one overwhelming moment.

It was sustained pressure.

And in that kind of environment, something becomes clear quickly:

You're not managing performance the same way anymore.

You're managing people.

There was frustration — not directed at anyone, but at the situation itself.

An extremely difficult hand to be dealt.

And yet, the expectation to lead didn't pause just because life had changed.

In those months, leadership became more relational than operational.

We could not gather easily. So I leaned into connection where I could.

We arranged boxed lunches for team members — small gestures, but meaningful ones when normal rhythms were gone. We checked in not just on numbers, but on families. We asked how people were holding up, not just how accounts were performing.

The conversations changed.

Less "Where are we against target?"

More "How are you doing?"

Standards shifted.

Not because we wanted them to.

Because reality demanded it.

The focus became steadiness.

Keep people safe.

Keep the team connected.

Keep moving forward where possible.

We simplified priorities even further.

What mattered most became clearer, because it had to.

Everything else could wait.

That season required a different kind of leadership.

Less direction.

More presence.

Even when that presence was virtual.

More patience.

More flexibility.

More grace.

And an acceptance that not every season is meant for acceleration.

Some are meant for endurance.

Looking back, that season didn't just test leadership.

It revealed it.

When structure weakens, character becomes more visible.

You can't rely on proximity.

You can't rely on routine.

You rely on trust.

And trust, in that season, was built differently.

Not through performance alone.

But through consistency, care, and presence when it mattered most.

10
Leading Humans, Not Metrics

Metrics matter.

Scorecards matter.

Execution standards matter.

Performance matters.

But metrics do not wake up in the morning and make decisions.

People do.

Early in my first leadership role, I believed that if I clearly communicated the objective, results would follow exactly as described. I underestimated something simple: I was not leading spreadsheets. I was leading humans.

Humans have thoughts.

Emotions.

Personal circumstances.

Strengths.

Blind spots.

Different ways of learning.

It was not enough to say, "Here is the goal — go execute."

Some learn by seeing.

Some learn by hearing.

Some need repetition.

Some need space.

Some need encouragement.

Some need challenge.

If you teach one way and assume everyone receives it the same way, you will always miss part of your team.

We had metrics that tracked both effort and outcomes. They revealed patterns.

But they did not reveal belief.

That required proximity.

Time in stores.

One-on-one conversations.

Listening beyond performance.

I stepped into one team where I wasn't sure what I had.

We were all learning each other.

I didn't know how we would mesh.

I didn't know if we would meet expectations.

And if I'm honest, I wondered early on whether we had a true "go-to" player — someone who could consistently lead from the front.

I was wrong.

We had several.

One in particular stood out over time.

Their reputation coming in was mixed.

Not because of their effort or ability, but because of the environments they had been placed in before. Challenging roles. Difficult circumstances. Situations that shaped perception more than performance.

Guilt by association.

But once I spent time with them, a different picture emerged.

They were capable.

Engaged.

Willing.

What they lacked wasn't ability.

It was belief.

So I started to challenge them.

Not aggressively.

Intentionally.

Pushing where I saw opportunity.

Holding a higher standard.

Expecting more — not because they were failing, but because they were capable of more.

And something started to happen.

The more I challenged, the more they responded.

It wasn't forced.

It built.

Confidence started to show up where hesitation used to be.

Decisions became clearer.

Execution became sharper.

Results followed.

Not gradually.

Quickly.

That shift didn't come from a metric.

It came from unlocking belief.

Over time, others started to see it too.

Leadership's view changed.

The same person who had once been seen through the lens of prior circumstances was now viewed as a leader on the team.

A top performer.

Someone positioned for multiple opportunities ahead.

That experience reinforced something I had been learning:

People are not reputations.

They are potential — often waiting to be recognized, challenged, and developed.

Metrics can tell you what is happening.

They rarely tell you why.

That requires time.

It requires attention.

It requires a willingness to see beyond what is immediately visible.

I often asked simple questions:

What's going well?

Where do you feel stuck?

If you were in my position, what decision would you make here?

That last question mattered.

It shifted ownership.

It revealed how someone was thinking — not just how they were performing.

I have had many team members promoted over the years. That has been one of the most meaningful measures of success for me.

I know I would not be where I am without leaders who spoke my name in rooms I was not in — leaders who pushed me, corrected me, and believed in me.

There was a time when I saw the team I led as a vehicle to get me where I wanted to go.

That perspective changed.

My growth was directly tied to their growth.

Helping them advance strengthened my own development.

Stewarding their opportunity strengthened mine.

Leadership is not about leveraging people.

It is about investing in them.

Metrics measure output.

Leadership measures impact.

11
Alignment Over Acceleration

There is a subtle temptation in leadership to measure progress by movement.

How quickly did you advance?

How rapidly did circumstances change?

How soon did recognition follow?

But movement alone is not evidence of direction.

Earlier in my career, I often asked for doors to open. I prepared, performed, and pursued. When opportunities stalled, I pushed harder.

At that point in my life, I didn't think much about alignment.

I leaned on free will.

On effort.

On the belief that if I worked hard enough and made the right moves, the outcome would follow.

Looking back, the idea that I was in full control seems almost laughable.

But I wasn't mature enough in my faith to see it that way at the time.

So I kept pushing.

Over time, something began to shift.

Not all at once.

Gradually.

Instead of asking for my plans to succeed, I began asking a different question:

Is this aligned?

That shift didn't eliminate effort.

It redirected it.

I still prepared.

I still pursued.

But I became more aware of what I was pursuing—and why.

I started to pray differently.

Not just about major decisions.

About everything.

Big things.

Small things.

All things.

Because I came to a realization that changed how I approached leadership and life:

I don't want a thing that isn't aligned with God's plan and purpose.

That changed how I viewed opportunity.

Before, I evaluated what was available.

Now, I considered what was aligned.

That distinction matters.

Because access is not the same as alignment.

Just because something is in front of you does not mean it is meant for you.

Acceleration, detached from alignment, often leads to outcomes that don't last.

Or outcomes that come at a cost you didn't anticipate.

Alignment requires something different.

It requires patience.

It requires trust.

And it requires a willingness to surrender control.

Not of effort—but of outcome.

Looking back across seasons of rejection, growth, correction, and opportunity, a pattern becomes clear.

Not a formula.

Not a strategy.

A posture.

One that continues to be refined.

Stewarded influence has required:

Formation over performance.

Clarity over noise.

Steadiness over volatility.

Investment over leverage.

Alignment over acceleration.

None of these were mastered quickly.

All were formed over time.

And I remain in that formation still.

EPILOGUE

The Quiet Work

Leadership rarely feels dramatic while you are living it.

It feels like early mornings and long drives. Difficult conversations and quiet preparation. The weight of decisions that linger long after meetings end.

And at times, it feels lonely.

Not because you are isolated from people, but because responsibility rests differently on you. Decisions carry weight. Words matter more. You absorb tension so others can focus. You process privately so conversations can remain productive.

Much of that work happens unseen.

Over time, my perspective on leadership has changed.

What once felt like a role has become something different.

It feels like a calling.

An opportunity.

Not something I have to do—but something I get to do.

Less about holding responsibility.

More about stewarding it.

Less about keeping what I've learned.

More about passing it on.

Investing in younger colleagues. Developing them intentionally. Not because it's required—but because it matters.

Because someone once did that for me.

That shift changes how you show up.

It changes how you listen.

It changes how you lead.

I have been grateful to never carry that weight alone.

We talk daily — about schedules, responsibilities, and the ordinary rhythms of life. But when significant moments approach — when conversations carry weight, when decisions require clarity — I turn to my wife.

She has shaped me in ways I did not expect when we first started this journey.

In how she leads.

In how she follows.

In how she sacrifices.

In how she listens.

She sees things differently than I do.

She hears what I might miss.

She asks questions that slow me down and bring clarity before I ever step into a room.

She has helped refine not just what I say—but how I say it.

And how it will be received.

Those conversations have become part of my leadership process.

They ground me.

They steady me.

They remind me that leadership is not just about direction.

It is about understanding.

It is about awareness.

It is about people.

One of the lessons that has become clearer over time is this:

You have to know how to follow to be able to lead.

And you have to lead with purpose and alignment—or it won't work.

Not long term.

Not in a way that lasts.

Much of leadership remains unseen.

You rarely know which conversation will anchor someone. Which moment of composure will carry more weight than volume ever could. Which quiet act of integrity will outlast a season.

So you show up.

You stay steady.

You keep learning.

Over time, patterns form. Trust deepens. Credibility strengthens. Confidence steadies.

Not because you were flawless.

But because you were faithful.

Long after titles shift and seasons close, what remains is how you carried responsibility — and who you became while doing so.

That is the quiet work.

And over time, it endures.

ABOUT THE AUTHOR

Kevin Horton is a corporate leader with more than two decades of experience guiding teams through growth, pressure, and change. Over the course of his career, he has led diverse teams across multiple markets, navigating both performance-driven environments and seasons that required steadiness beyond metrics.

Grounded in his Christian faith, Kevin believes influence is not something to accumulate, but something to steward — faithfully, patiently, and with humility. His leadership philosophy has been shaped as much by correction and formation as by achievement and advancement. He writes about leadership not from theory, but from lived experience — from rejection, responsibility, recalibration, and growth.

Kevin is passionate about developing people and building cultures defined by clarity, accountability, and character. Many of the leaders he has worked alongside have gone on to earn expanded opportunities, a reflection of his belief that leadership is measured by who grows because of it.

He lives in Georgia with his wife and son and continues to learn what it means to lead with conviction, humility, and steady purpose.